D1307503

UNSOLVED MYSTERIES

the secret files

The Loch Ness Monster

Martin Delrio

the rosen publishing group's

rosen central

To the scientists of the world,
seeking truth in confusing data

Published in 2002 by The Rosen Publishing Group, Inc.
29 East 21st Street, New York, NY 10010

Copyright © 2002 by The Rosen Publishing Group, Inc.

First Edition

All rights reserved. No part of this book may be reproduced in any form without permission in writing from the publisher, except by a reviewer.

Library of Congress Cataloging-in-Publication Data

Delrio, Martin.
The Loch Ness monster / by Martin Delrio.
p. cm. — (Unsolved mysteries)
Includes bibliographical references.
Summary: Examines the origins of Loch Ness, stories about the monster first reported to dwell there in 565 A.D., eyewitness reports and photographic evidence, recent scientific investigations, and possible explanations.
ISBN 0-8239-3564-7 (library binding)
1. Loch Ness monster—Juvenile literature. [1. Loch Ness monster. 2. Monsters.] I. Title. II. Unsolved mysteries (Rosen Publishing Group)
QL89.2.L6 D46 2002
001.944—dc21

2001005391

Manufactured in the United States of America

Contents

The Loch Ness monster is another incarnation of the great sea serpent that humans have almost always feared existed.

Introduction

Let no one imagine that I either state a falsehood . . . or record anything doubtful or uncertain. Be it known that I will tell with all candor what I have learned from the consistent narrative of my predecessors, trustworthy and discerning men, and that my narrative is founded either on what I have been able to find recorded in the pages of those who have gone before me, or what I have learned in diligent inquiry, by hearing it from certain faithful old men, who have told me without hesitation.

—St. Adamnan,
Life of St. Columba

1
Earliest Sighting

Far up in the north of Great Britain, surrounded by the rugged mountains of the Scottish Highlands, lies Loch Ness. Is this cold, dark lake the natural habitat of a huge creature not yet known to zoologists? Or—as skeptics maintain—is there nothing to back up the reported sightings but hysteria, bad science, and wishful thinking?

The story of the Loch Ness monster begins more than fourteen hundred years ago, in AD 565. In that year, the Irish missionary Saint Columba had a dramatic encounter with a water monster. Columba's biographer, Saint Adamnan, tells the story:

On another occasion also, when the blessed man was living for some days in the province of the Picts, he was

Early accounts of the Loch Ness monster described a mighty sea creature that preyed on people at sea.

obliged to cross the river Ness; and when he reached the bank of the river, he saw some of the inhabitants burying an unfortunate man, who was a short time before seized as he was swimming, and bitten most severely by a monster that lived in the water . . . The blessed man, on hearing this . . . directed one of his companions to swim over and row across the boat that was moored at the farther bank . . .

But the monster, which, so far from being satiated, was only roused for more prey, was lying at the bottom of the stream, and when it felt the water disturbed above by the man swimming, suddenly rushed out and, giving an awful roar, darted after him with its mouth wide open, as the man swam in the middle of the stream. Then the blessed man observing this, raised his holy hand . . . and commanded the ferocious monster, saying, "Thou shalt go no further, nor touch the man; go back with all speed." Then at the voice of the saint, the monster was terrified, and fled more quickly than if it had been pulled back with ropes.

Adamnan's story is interesting—but is it true? Adamnan himself undoubtedly believed it. But Adamnan wrote his *Life of St. Columba* over a century after Columba's supposed meeting with the water monster.

Also, the monster seen by Columba is different in at least two ways from the creature described in modern reports. Columba's monster makes "an awful roar," and it is a killer. The modern Loch Ness monster, on the other hand, makes no sounds

The legendary kelpie, or "water horse" preceded the Loch Ness monster by hundreds of years.

and doesn't attack people. All that the story really tells us is that reports of a lake (or river) monster near Loch Ness go back at least as far as the sixth century.

Legends of water monsters were well known in the Highlands of Scotland. The kelpie, also known as the water-horse, was a creature that lived in and about the lochs. The name "water-horse" came from its habit of taking the appearance of a fine horse standing saddled and bridled by the roadside. Unfortunate travelers who tried to ride this horse would find themselves stuck on its back, unable to let loose of the rein, as the creature plunged headlong into the nearby loch.

With the coming of the modern era, the stories about the Highland water-horses grew less fantastical and more realistic.

Gone were the enchanted bridles and the death plunges, but from time to time the occasional sighting of an unusual animal would still be reported in the local press.

For example, in 1802, a man named Alexander Macdonald saw a large stubby-legged animal surface and propel itself to within fifty yards of where he stood on the shore of the loch. In 1880, another Macdonald—named Duncan this time—dove into the loch near Fort Augustus to inspect the keel of a wrecked ship. While he was down there, he saw an animal like a huge frog lying on an underwater shelf of rock. And in 1926, the *Inverness Courier* reported that a Mr. Simon McGarry of Invergarry saw the gulls rise screaming into the air above the loch, and a creature emerge. "Before my eyes, something like an upturned boat rose from the depths, and I can still see the water cascading down its sides. Just as suddenly, though, it sank out of sight."

Then, in 1933, a Highlander named Hugh Gray was walking beside the river near the village of Foyers when he saw a creature rolling about in the water. But this encounter was different from all the rest. Hugh Gray was carrying a camera.

2
A Bit of Background

Four hundred million years ago, in what would someday become the Scottish Highlands, part of the Caledonian Mountains slid more than sixty miles to the south. The fault line left a mile-wide rift valley that still runs all the way across Scotland, from the North Sea to the Atlantic Ocean. This valley is Glen Mor, the Great Glen. Loch Ness lies in the northeasternmost portion of the Great Glen.

Over time, the continents cracked apart and drifted. During the age of dinosaurs, long-necked plesiosaurs swam in the shallow seas that covered much of North America and Europe. Mammals arose, dinosaurs died off, the climate grew colder, and eventually ice sheets spread over much of the world.

During the ice ages, glaciers covered the Scottish Highlands with a layer of ice up to 4,000 feet deep. The ice pressed down on the land and caused the rock to sink beneath sea level. As the ice melted,

Glen Mor, the Great Glen of Scotland, is geologically active with approximately three major earthquakes per century.

the land rose. The portion of the rift valley that would become Loch Ness was an arm of the sea. The rising land, the falling sea level, and the melting glaciers worked together to cut off the loch from the ocean and replace the salt water with fresh water. The surface of the loch is now about fifty-two feet above sea level.

Loch Ness today is the largest of a series of glacial lakes running along the fault line of the Great Glen from Inverness to Fort William. At 22.5 miles long by 1.75 miles wide at its widest point, with a depth of over 750 feet, Loch Ness holds the greatest volume of fresh water in Great Britain.

The sides of the loch are steep, and the bottom of the loch is soft mud, flat and level. The rock walls of the loch extend below the mud in a V shape and may go down as far as 900 feet. Not counting the mud and whatever lies below it, Loch Ness is the second-deepest lake in the British Isles, and the third-deepest lake in Europe. The River Ness, about seven miles long, drains the loch into the sea at Beauly Firth. The Highland city of Inverness is located on the river, between Loch Ness and the sea.

The waters of Loch Ness are dark and cold, and murky with particles of peat moss washed in by the streams that feed the loch. The sun warms the upper levels of the loch, down to about 150 feet. Below 150 feet, the water maintains a constant temperature near 45 degrees Fahrenheit. The loch never freezes over, even in the coldest Highland winters.

Humans came into the Great Glen area around 6,000 years ago. The first settlers were the Picts, whose name comes from the Latin *picti*, or "painted people," a nickname the Romans gave them because of their fondness for tattoos and body paint.

From the Middle Ages on through the beginning of the modern era, war and violence marked the countryside around the loch. In the eleventh century, Macbeth supposedly murdered King Duncan while the king was a guest at Macbeth's castle about a half-mile northeast of Inverness. Bonnie Prince Charlie's defeat in 1746 at the Battle of Culloden, seven miles south of Inverness, spelled the end of Scottish independence.

Workers on the Caledonian Canal, which runs through Loch Ness, reportedly saw a "creature" in the loch.

Over the next century, modern agriculture and the desire for wealth finished what warfare had started. For centuries the Highlanders had lived by small-scale agriculture and cattle raising, but in the late 1700s the great landowners began changing over to large-scale sheep farming. To make room for flocks of sheep, the landowners forcibly evicted their own tenant farmers. The Highland Clearances, as the process was called, lasted into the nineteenth century.

The Caledonian Canal, begun in 1803, opened the Great Glen to commerce. By the early years of the twentieth century, Inverness had become a popular tourist destination, reachable by train. In 1933—the same year that Hugh Gray took his walk by the river—the Loch Ness road finally opened the banks of the loch to automobile traffic.

3
A Monster Takes Shape

s there a large animal in Loch Ness? Between the time when St. Columba dismissed a monster with his word and when Hugh Gray snapped his photo, there were perhaps two dozen mentions of a creature in the loch. The monster usually takes one of three forms. The first and most common is the moving wake, a pattern of waves in the water of the loch that hints at the presence of something large swimming just beneath. The second is a humped body, either moving or stationary, rising above the water. The third and rarest form is a long neck with a small head.

Could, however, an undiscovered animal as large as the Loch Ness monster possibly exist? The answer is yes. Animals previously unknown to science have been found more than once in the past hundred years. For instance, there's the megamouth shark (*megachasma pelagios*), a fifteen-foot-long creature weighing nearly a ton. The first specimen was discovered on November 15, 1976,

A megamouth shark found dead on the shore of a beach in Cagayan de Oro City, Philippines, in 1998. No one suspected that the megamouth shark existed before 1976.

when it was found entangled in the drag anchor of a U.S. Navy ship. The new creature wasn't described scientifically until 1983. Twelve years after the first sighting, only three specimens had been found. Since that time, fewer than twenty megamouth sharks have been captured, or even seen. The megamouth remains the only species in its genus, and the only genus in its order.

There's also the pseudo-oryx, a large antelope discovered in Southeast Asia in 1992. Local inhabitants, of course, had always known about the animal. It was merely the mainstream of

The coelacanth was thought to be extinct until a living specimen was caught in 1938.

science that hadn't gotten the word. Other animals once thought to be legendary that have been proved to exist within the last hundred years include the giant panda and the Kodiak bear.

Sometimes, creatures thought to have vanished long ago have been rediscovered. The coelacanth, an ancient fish, was known only from the fossil record. Scientists thought that the species had died out some 400 million years ago. Then, in 1938, a fisherman caught a coelacanth off the coast of Africa. A second one turned up in 1952, and others have been seen since.

Could the reports of a Loch Ness monster be a case of the implausible being true? Let's take a look at some evidence.

On July 22, 1930, three young men from Inverness were fishing from a boat near Dores. They sighted a disturbance in the water about 600 yards away from them, moving toward them at about 15 knots (17 miles per hour) until it came to within 300 yards, with a part protruding from the water being twenty feet long by three feet high.

On April 14, 1933, Mr. and Mrs. John Mackay were driving along the side of Loch Ness on the recently completed auto road from Inverness. Near the town of Abriachan, Mrs. Mackay spotted "an enormous animal rolling and plunging" in the center of the loch.

The *Daily Express,* a Glasgow newspaper, reported on June 9, 1933: "Mystery fish in Scottish loch. Monster reported at Fort Augustus. A monster fish which for years has been somewhat of a mystery in Loch Ness was reported to have been seen yesterday at Fort Augustus."

On October 23, 1933, the *Daily Mail,* a London newspaper, reported from Scotland: "In Inverness, the Highland Capital, there is one topic of conversation—'the beast' as by one accord everybody dubs the uncanny denizen of the loch by this sinister title. Some think the loch harbors a survivor of some prehistoric creature which may have been released from the earth's recesses by the great blasting operations required for the making of the new Inverness-Glasgow motor road."

On October 29, 1933, Mr. E. G. Boulenger, the director of the aquarium at the London Zoo, sounded a word of caution: "The case of the Monster in Loch Ness is worthy of our consideration if only because it presents a striking example of mass hallucination."

On November 13, 1933, the same day on which Mr. Gray snapped his photo, the government became involved. Sir Murdoch Macdonald, representing Inverness-shire in Parliament, wrote to the secretary of state for Scotland, "As no doubt you are aware, some animal or fish of an unusual kind has found its way into Loch Ness. I think I can say the evidence of its presence can be taken as undoubted. Far too many people have seen something abnormal to question its existence. So far, there has been no indication of its being a harmful animal or fish, and until somebody states the genus to which it belongs, I do hope you can authorise the police in the district to prevent pothunters deliberately looking for it."

But the tales of the Loch Ness monster proved to be more than just a seven-day wonder and a silly-season newspaper flash. By one count, over 4,000 eyewitness accounts of an unusual animal in Loch Ness have appeared since 1933, eleven of them in 2000.

4

The Case of the Mysterious Photos

Loch Ness is big—one and a half miles wide and twenty-four miles long. An observer standing at the waterline and looking across the loch will find that the opposite shore is halfway to the horizon. Looking lengthwise down the loch, the same observer would not be able to see the far end at all.

Weather conditions at the loch are extreme. The weather station at Fort Augustus, in the period between 1920 and 1950, reported fewer sunny days than any other station in Britain. The wind howls up the Great Glen, whipping the surface of the loch to foam where a moment before the water had been still and glassy. Observation is even trickier during twilight, and the high northern latitude of Scotland produces long twilights.

Making observations across open water is difficult at best. Estimating size and distance is hard without familiar objects near the unknown to provide scale. Open water is also prone to mirage conditions. A floating log, a bird, a distant boat, a windblown wave, a deer swimming in the loch—any of these things, seen under the right lighting conditions, could be misinterpreted as a fabulous monster. Furthermore, human memories are fallible. People see what they want to see and remember what they want to remember. We must turn, then, to the photos of the Loch Ness monster for our evidence.

Let's consider Hugh Gray's photo first. It is, at best, a blurry shot of something unidentifiable. There are no foreground objects with which to make a size comparison. Mr. Gray estimated the object to be 200 yards away. An ordinary camera is hard-pressed to take detailed photos at that range. Mr. Gray stated that the object was obscured by spray, that it was dark gray in color, and that it stood three to four feet out of the water. He took five shots with his camera, then went home.

Hugh Gray's photo of the Loch Ness monster

And there his camera, with what could be astounding pictures inside, lay untouched for two weeks. The most charitable interpretation of this delay is the one Mr. Gray himself gives: He was afraid that nothing would appear on the film and that he would be kidded by his fellow workers. When the film was at last developed, four of the five shots showed nothing, and the fifth showed what seemed to be a creature with its head under water, the tail farthest from the photographer.

A less charitable interpretation is that there was no creature at all and that it was only after seeing a blurred and indistinct picture on the developed film that Mr. Gray came up with a story to sell to the press. Some people who look at the photo see the head of a dog with a stick in its mouth, swimming toward the camera. Other researchers see other creatures, which all seem to fit the various theories about the monster.

Matters were not helped when the next piece of hard evidence turned out to be a provable hoax. The *Daily Mail* hired a professional big-game hunter to go to Loch Ness and bring back evidence of the creature's existence. The hunter, Mr. Marmaduke "Duke" Wetherall, arrived in mid-December

This underwater photo was submitted in 1975 to prove the monster exists.

1933. Within a few days, Mr. Wetherall had found mysterious footprints on the shores of the loch. He dutifully made a plaster cast and sent it back to London for identification, all amidst great publicity. And amid great publicity came the answer, issued from the British Museum of Natural History on January 4, 1934: The footprints were all made by the right rear foot of a female hippopotamus. Stuffed.

Someone had apparently used a hippopotamus-foot umbrella stand to create the "monster" footprints, and Mr. Wetherall had fallen for it.

Instantly, the Loch Ness monster became a laughingstock that no legitimate scientist could touch and come away with his reputation intact. Forty years later, when the Academy of Applied Science launched an expedition to the loch in an attempt to take underwater photos of the creature, they would be mocked by the comic strip *Doonesbury* as "the Academy of Implied Science."

Mr. Wetherall stated that in his opinion the loch contained nothing more than a large gray seal. The publicity started to fade.

Then came April 1934. On the nineteenth of that month, R. K. Wilson, a respected London surgeon, was on holiday in Scotland. Around 7:00 in the morning, Mr. Wilson stopped about two miles north of Invermoriston. He said, "I had got over the dyke and was standing a few yards down the slope and looking towards the loch when I noticed a considerable commotion on the surface some distance out from the shore, perhaps two or three hundred yards out. I watched it for perhaps a minute or so and saw something break the surface. My friend shouted: 'My God, it's the Monster!'

"I ran the few yards to the car and got the camera and then went down and along the steep bank for about fifty yards to where my friend was and got the camera focused on something which was moving through the water. I could not say what this object was as I was far too busy managing the camera in my amateurish way."

This is one of the most famous
photos of what some say is the
Loch Ness monster.

Mr. Wilson shot four photos, which he took to have developed that same day in Inverness. The pictures came back that afternoon. The first two were blank; the third showed what appeared to be a head and neck rising above the water. The fourth showed the creature sinking back into the loch.

That third and best-known photo is certainly startling. If this is indeed the head and neck of a creature extending four feet above the surface of the loch, it resembles nothing so much as a plesiosaur, a carnivorous aquatic reptile thought to have become extinct some 65 million years ago.

5

The Mystery Deepens

Mr. Wilson sold the head-and-neck picture to the *Daily Mail* on his return to London and created an instant sensation. For some people, the photograph proved the existence of an unknown animal. Others weren't so sure.

When a picture of an unknown object has no objects of known size in the foreground, the exact size of the unknown object can't be determined. In this case, rather than seeing a large object from afar, some people saw a small object close by: a water bird, the tail of a diving otter, a floating log with a root sticking above the water.

One of the objections to the photo is that while Mr. Wilson said that the thing he photographed was moving, the ripples on the water show it to be stationary. Perhaps, some say, it was moving but had stopped by the time he got his camera to his eye. Perhaps, others suggest, it was never moving at all.

The second photo, the one the newspaper didn't run, is of far poorer quality than the famous shot. Nevertheless, it has some

Loch Ness, twice as deep as the North Sea, contains more water than the rest of the lakes of the British Isles combined.

interesting features. One is that the angle between the "head" and the "neck" of the object has changed. It's unlikely that a tree root would make such a change.

And there matters remained until 1994. On March 13 of that year, the *Sunday Telegraph* ran a story claiming that the famous photo was actually a picture of an eighteen-inch model, and that Mr. Wilson had not taken the photos himself, but had allowed his name and reputation to be used for the occasion. According to the *Sunday Telegraph*, a man named Christian Spurling had confessed to perpetrating a hoax sixty years before at the urging of his stepfather—none other than Duke Wetherall, the big-game hunter who had himself been hoaxed by the stuffed hippo foot.

By the time Mr. Spurling told his story, everyone else supposedly involved in the hoax was dead. And by the time the story was printed, Mr. Spurling himself was dead at the age of ninety. All anyone can say for certain, therefore, is that either Mr. Spurling was fibbing, or Mr. Wilson was.

What do we know scientifically? Science works, first, by collecting the available information, or data, about the thing being studied. Second, scientists take this information and try to come up with a hypothesis that explains how the data fits together. Third, they devise experiments to test the hypothesis. Once a hypothesis is verified by the experimental method, it becomes a theory.

Along the way there are several general principles. One is called Occam's razor, after William of Occam, a medieval monk and early scientist who said, "Logical entities should not be multiplied unnecessarily." Another way of putting that is, "If you have two competing theories that make exactly the same predictions, the one that is simpler is the better."

The least-complex theory may still be quite complex. As Albert Einstein put it, "Everything should be made as simple as possible, but not simpler."

Given two hypotheses, one that "the sightings of unidentified objects in Loch Ness are caused by unknown animals seen at great distances under bad light conditions," and the second that "the sightings of unidentified objects in Loch Ness are caused by floating logs seen at great distances under bad light conditions," the log explanation is simpler. We already know, by other means, that there are floating logs in the loch.

Is there a reasonable way to prove that the loch (or, indeed, any body of water) is monster-free? If a search fails to find any monsters, then perhaps the search was in the wrong location, at the wrong time, or using the wrong means. If one photo turns out to be a fake, that doesn't mean that the next photo won't be real. If one observer is mistaken, that doesn't mean the next observer won't be completely accurate. The people who claim that there is a large, unknown animal in Loch Ness are the ones who have to provide the proof that there really is one. Extraordinary claims require extraordinary proof.

Show us the proof, the skeptics say. Give us a monster we can study in the flesh.

6
Hunting for Nessie

The history of the Loch Ness monster continued after R. K. Wilson sold his picture to the *Daily Mail*. In the summer of 1934, Sir Edward Mountain, a gentleman described as "an enthusiastic angler," rented Beaufort Castle on Loch Ness and spent the month of July hunting for evidence of a creature. He hired twenty men and posted them a mile or so apart down the twenty-four-mile length of the loch. Each man had binoculars and a camera, and watched from 8 AM to 6 PM. The men reported back every night on what they had seen. Sir Edward marked each sighting on a map of the loch. In two weeks of good weather, the watchers claimed to have sighted what could be a creature no fewer than twenty-one times, and took five photos. Then bad weather set in, and the sightings stopped. The five photos were "disappointing," lacking even the detail of the London surgeon's photo. No conclusions could be drawn.

A team from the Loch Ness Monster Investigation Bureau scanned the loch for a monster sighting in 1968.

Sir Edward switched to one man with a movie camera and a telephoto lens. This eventually yielded movie footage of something later identified by zoologists as a large seal, the same conclusion that Duke Wetherall had reached earlier. Sir Edward's film has since been lost.

During World War II, the loch came under the control of the Royal Navy. The monster was forgotten. Then in 1951, a worker for the Forestry Commission named Lachlan Steuart saw what he first thought was a large motorboat speeding down the loch. Realizing that it was no motorboat, he grabbed a camera and took a photograph of a three-humped creature that he estimated to be about fifty-seven feet long from nose to tail.

The kind of creature that might have such a shape is difficult to imagine. Some people see not one creature, but three in a pack traveling together. Others claim that the photo shows three hay bales floating in the loch, and that Mr. Steuart was either mistaken or fibbing when he claimed that he saw them move.

There matters might have stood, but new evidence from another source turned up. On December 2, 1954, a fishing boat named *Rival III* out of Peterhead was passing down the loch when something unusual turned up on the echosounder. The device showed an object off Urquhart Bay, 480 feet down, 120 feet above the bottom of the loch. Experts who later examined the trace stated that the echo wasn't the result of a mechanical malfunction from the machine, that it hadn't been tampered with, and that the object wasn't a waterlogged tree or a school of fish.

More sonar evidence turned up over the following years. In 1968, the University of Birmingham, using shore-mounted sonar, detected and recorded a large unknown object traveling in the loch.

Some sonar searches have been disappointing. If identifying an animal from a blurry photograph is difficult, identifying one from a sonar echo is more so. The nearly vertical, parallel stone sides of Loch Ness, combined with the thermocline (a boundary between water layers of different temperatures) at 150 feet down, produce difficult conditions for sonar operation. Sonar signals are bent or reflected when they hit a thermocline.

In 1976, Christopher McGowan and Martin Klein searched the bottom of Loch Ness for the bones of a monster, using towed side-scan sonar. The system had found mastodon bones on the bottom of a lake in New Hampshire during a test run. But, while they found the remains of a crashed World War II aircraft in Loch Ness, and Pictish stone circles beneath the current waterline, no monster bones turned up. However, McGowan and Klein searched only the shallow areas of the loch.

In 1982, months of patrolling with scanning sonar produced forty hits on objects larger than the largest known fish, which could not be explained as false signals.

In 1987, Operation Deepscan was mounted. It consisted of nineteen boats moving side by side, sweeping the loch from wall to

Boats with "creature cameras" line the span of the loch in an ambitious search for the monster.

wall with a curtain of sound. They sailed the long way down the loch, once each way, during the two-day search. Numerous strong sonar echoes "larger than a shark but smaller than a whale" were recorded. They all appeared to be moving, and many were below 150 feet. Yet problems abounded with this search, too. The sonar systems mounted on the boats interfered with each other, so they had to be set to their lowest power. At the end of the two-day sweep, all the expedition organizers had was a set of returns that they couldn't identify.

Sonar continues to be used to search the loch, although with inconclusive results. We know a lot more about the loch now; for instance, we know that the water under the thermocline, once thought to be devoid of life, actually has an 80 percent oxygen saturation, and that fish live there down to the bottom, where arctic char and lampreys swim in the blackness. But so far, no unknown animals have been brought to the surface.

While the sonar searches went on, surface observation and photography continued. In 1960, a man named Tim Dinsdale took a movie of an unknown object in the loch. Some claim that it was a motorboat seen at a great distance under poor lighting conditions. But when the film was analyzed by Britain's Joint Air Reconnaissance Intelligence Center (JARIC) in 1966, the RAF's photographic experts said that what the film showed was "probably an animate object."

During the years 1962–1972, a group called the Loch Ness Phenomena Investigation Bureau ringed the loch with movie and still cameras fitted with telephoto lenses in an attempt to duplicate one or more of the classic monster photos. While they did get some photos of objects that could not be identified, they did not get any photos of objects that were definitely an unknown animal.

The Academy of Applied Sciences, an American group, launched an investigation of its own in the early 1970s, financed in part by the *New York Times* and the National Geographic Society. The expedition was led by Dr. Robert Rines. The equipment was designed by Harold "Doc" Edgerton, a professor at Massachusetts Institute of Technology and the inventor of both strobe photography and side-scan sonar. When computer enhanced, the underwater photos they took seemed to show a large, five-sided fin, and—in another photo—the head and neck of an unknown animal.

"None of the photographs is sufficiently informative to establish the existence, far less the identity, of a large animal in the loch," a team of experts from the British Museum of Natural History said in November 1975. "To one of us it strongly suggested the head of a horse with a bridle, and others conceded this likeness when it was pointed out. The size limits are compatible with this explanation. On this

The "creature camera" operated remotely once deployed from a boat.

interpretation, eyes, ears, noseband, and nostrils are visible, along with a less clear structure that could represent a neck. We believe that the image is too imprecise for us to argue that this does indeed represent a dead horse, but we equally believe that such an interpretation cannot be eliminated."

Unfortunately, the murky water of the loch made the underwater photos blurry and dim, and when others tried to computer enhance the original photos, they did not get the same results that the academy did. Other investigations followed, using sonar, with surface and subsurface cameras, and even with small submarines. In the summer of 2000, a Swedish businessman asked for permission to cruise the loch with a specially modified crossbow, in an attempt to get a skin sample from the unknown animal, so that DNA testing could show what it was. He was refused permission on the grounds that Scottish law forbids annoying livestock.

What, then, is in Loch Ness? Hypotheses abound. None of them are strong enough to make it up to the status of theory. Assuming there is a creature, is it a mammal? Whales, seals, and giant otters have all been suggested, but sea mammals tend to be friendly and gregarious. They come up frequently for air, and on cold

Some investigators think the dark portion of this photograph shows disturbed water caused by the Loch Ness monster.

days their breath is visible. A family of whales spouting in the loch wouldn't remain mysterious for long.

How about a reptile? The extinct plesiosaur looks like the Loch Ness monster of legend. The water in the loch is cold, but it never freezes, and the leatherback turtle, an ocean-dwelling reptile, lives in the waters off Scotland. But reptiles also need to come to the surface for air. Furthermore, it would be astonishing if a breeding population of plesiosaurs had survived undetected for 65 million years.

An amphibian, then? Amphibians' bodies sink when they die, and some amphibians maintain gills all their lives. They might never need to come to the surface. Duncan Macdonald, the diver who saw something under water in 1880, described what he saw as looking like a frog. But amphibians lay egg masses, and no such eggs have been seen in the loch.

How about a fish? Sturgeon can grow quite large, and they are certainly odd-looking creatures. But sturgeon don't have long necks or a tendency to come to the surface.

A large invertebrate, with no fixed body shape, could supply the wide variety of forms attributed to the Loch Ness monster. Some writers have suggested that the long "neck" of the Loch Ness creature is a single tentacle of a giant squid, raised above the surface for a moment. One researcher suggested that the Loch Ness creature is a "tully monster." Unfortunately, the tully monster, like the plesiosaur, is long extinct, and its largest fossil is only a few centimeters long.

Suppose there isn't a living creature at all? What else could people have been reporting? Boats and floating logs, seen at a great distance under poor lighting conditions, have been suggested, but these explanations don't explain the close-up sightings.

How about mirages? W. H. Lehn of the Department of Electrical Engineering at the University of Manitoba published an article, "Atmospheric Refraction and Lake Monsters," in *Science* magazine in 1979. He demonstrated that the refraction effect of layers of air at different temperatures could make logs and similar objects appear to stretch upward and transform into long-necked "monsters." Cold, deep Loch Ness is ideal for producing inversion layers of the kind that Lehn suggests. But mirages don't alarm seabirds, and they don't create moving wakes that break on the shore.

Something that might produce waves breaking on shore without wind or a passing boat is minor earthquake activity. Loch Ness is in an active geologic fault. A temblor could certainly alarm seabirds.

Others have speculated that the hump rising from the surface of the loch is a mat of rotting vegetation, lifted by

The ruins of Urquhart Castle overlook the dark, cold water of Loch Ness.

methane gas, which sinks again after the gas bubble bursts into the air. We do know that there are two areas on the bottom of the loch—one off Fort Augustus, one off Urquhart Castle—that produce methane. But no such mats of vegetation have washed ashore.

There is no reason to suppose that all the monster sightings have the same cause. Nor is there any reason to rule out a large, unknown animal as one of the causes. As of this moment, we just don't know. The Smithsonian Institute says: "Even though most scientists believe the likelihood of a monster is small, they keep an open mind as scientists should and wait for concrete proof in the form of skeletal evidence or the actual capture of such a creature." Until then, observers on the shore will keep on looking for a rippled wake, or a humped back, or a long-necked creature rising out of the depths —and the waters of Loch Ness will keep their secrets.

Natural philosophy is now one of the favourite studies of the Scottish nation and Loch Ness well deserves to be diligently studied.

—Dr. Samuel Johnson, 1773

Glossary

data Information about something being studied.

echosounder A device that locates underwater objects by bouncing sound waves off them.

experiment A scientific test.

Highlands The mountainous area of northern Scotland.

hypothesis A proposed idea of how data fits together.

kelpie A dangerous, horse-shaped water monster in Scottish folklore; also called a water-horse.

Loch Ness The third-deepest lake in Europe and possibly the home of one or more "monsters."

Nessie Nickname for the Loch Ness monster.

plesiosaur A long-necked aquatic dinosaur. It has been suggested that the Loch Ness monster might be one.

theory A hypothesis that has been verified by scientific experiments.

thermocline A boundary between water layers of different temperatures.

zoologist A scientist who studies animals.

For More Information

Due to the changing nature of Internet links, the Rosen Publishing Group, Inc., has developed an online list of Web sites related to the subject of this book. This site is updated regularly. Please use this link to access the list:

http://www.rosenlinks.com/um/lonm

For Further Reading

Baumann, Elwood D. *The Loch Ness Monster*. New York: Franklin Watts, Inc., 1972.

Corliss, William R. *The Sourcebook: Strange Life*. Glen Arm, MD: The Sourcebook Project, 1976.

Garinger, Alan. *Water Monsters: Great Mysteries: Opposing Viewpoints*. San Diego, CA: Greenhaven Press, 1991.

Harrison, Paul. *The Encyclopaedia of The Loch Ness Monster*. London: Robert Hale Ltd., 1999.

Mackal, Roy P. *The Monsters of Loch Ness*. Chicago: The Swallow Press, 1976.

Meredith, Dennis L. *Search at Loch Ness*. New York: Quadrangle/The New York Times Book Company, 1977.

Robertson, R. Macdonald. *Selected Highland Folktales*. Edinburgh and London: Oliver and Boyd, 1961.

Sweeney, James B. *Sea Monsters: A Collection of Eyewitness Accounts*. New York: David McKay Company, Inc, 1977.

Witchell, Nicholas. *The Loch Ness Story*. New York: Penguin Books, 1974.

Index

ABOUT THE AUTHOR

Martin Delrio has been a newspaper reporter, an intelligence analyst, and a scuba diver, in addition to his career as an author of young adult fiction. He has been fascinated by the Loch Ness monster ever since he read Constance Whyte's *More Than a Legend* as a boy. Marty visited Loch Ness some years ago, but, regretfully, didn't see the monster himself.

PHOTO CREDITS

Cover, pp. 4, 32 © Hulton/Archive by Getty Images; pp. 7, 14, 17, 39 © Bettmann/Corbis; p. 9 by Thomas Forget; p. 12 © The Image Bank by Getty Images; p. 16 © Reyna Pioquinto of the Bureau of Fisheries and Aquatic Resources (BFAR); p. 21 © Hugh Gray/courtesy of loch-ness.com; p. 23 © Academy of Applied Science; p. 25 © FPG by Getty Images; p. 27 © Jim Richardson/Corbis; p. 35 © Derek Colcough/loch-ness.org; p. 37 © Ralph White/Corbis; p. 41 © C. S. Gray/The Image Works by Getty Images.

SERIES DESIGN AND LAYOUT

Geri Giordano